W9-CMZ-013

Persuasive Speaking

Dixie Waldo

The National Forensic League · Library of Public Speaking and Debate

rosen publishing's
rosen central®

New York

I dedicate this book to Chris and Jason, who both support me with their confidence, friendship, and wisdom. They are truly outstanding coaches and wonderful friends.

Published in 2007 by The Rosen Publishing Group, Inc.
29 East 21st Street, New York, NY 10010

First Edition

Library of Congress Cataloging-in-Publication Data

Waldo, Dixie.
  Persuasive speaking / Dixie Waldo.
    p. cm. -- (The National Forensic League library of public speaking and debate)
  Includes bibliographical references and index.
  ISBN-10: 1-4042-1028-8   **3 1088 1004 2189 8**
  ISBN-13: 978-1-4042-1028-8 (library binding)
  1. Extemporaneous speaking. I. Title.
  PN4168.W35 2007
  808.5'1—dc22
                                        2006030575

Manufactured in the United States of America

The National Forensic League Honor Society promotes secondary school speech and debate activities and interscholastic competition as a means to develop a student's lifelong skills and values, as well as the public's awareness of the value of speech, debate, and communication education.

The organization serves as the central agent for coordination and facilitation of:

- heightened public awareness of the value of speech communication skills;
- development of educational initiatives for student and teacher training;
- excellence in interscholastic competition;
- the promotion of honor society ideals.

As an organization, the National Forensic League embraces diversity, interconnection, and visionary leadership. The National Forensic League empowers students to become effective communicators, ethical individuals, critical thinkers, and leaders in a democratic society.

To learn more about starting a National Forensic League or National Junior Forensic League program at the middle or high school level, or to locate more resources on speech and/or debate, please contact National Forensic League, 125 Watson Street, Ripon, WI 54971, (920) 748-6206, or visit our Web site at **www.nflonline.org**.

Contents

Chapter 1

Persuasive and Extemporaneous Speaking

Should downloading music be a crime?
Should students be required to pass standardized tests in order to graduate?
Is alternative rock superior to classic rock?

Questions like these spark great conversations between friends. If we answer these questions reasonably and with enthusiasm, we may be able to change a person's point of view. Clearly understanding the issues surrounding these topics is essential for creating persuasive answers as well.

You try to persuade people to agree with you every day without even thinking about it. You persuade your mom to let you have a cookie before dinner. You persuade your brother to let you borrow his sweater. You may even persuade your teacher to give you an extra day with an assignment.

Persuasion is a method by which we try to convince others to agree with us. Persuading others requires more than just effective speaking skills. You must also understand the opposition before you can construct a strong argument or offer a good solution to a problem.

You've probably already been introduced to persuasive writing in school. Perhaps you've learned how to write a persuasive essay. Maybe you've even read your essay aloud in class. This book will reinforce what you've learned and offer advice about how to be a successful persuasive speaker. You'll explore the elements of a well-crafted persuasive argument and learn how to find research to support a point of view. You'll also be introduced to a form of competitive public speaking called extemporaneous speaking.

Extemporaneous speaking is an activity in which a speaker is given a short amount of time to prepare a persuasive speech for an audience. Competitive extemporaneous speakers usually address current issues and events. These speakers develop self-confidence and learn skills that help them throughout their lives.

Chapter 2

Appealing to the Audience

Whether you're speaking to classmates or to a judge in a round of competition, public speaking requires that you consider your audience. People with thoughts and feelings are listening to what you are saying. You must keep these people in mind while speaking.

For an audience of classmates, you might tell a joke or talk about a popular school topic. In front of adults, you might speak more formally about an interesting political topic. You probably consider your audience in informal situations without even realizing it. Think of how you speak to a group of teachers compared with how you speak to a group of friends. Audience consideration becomes even more important in competitive speaking.

The ancient Greek philosopher Aristotle taught the art of public speaking and reasoning. Aristotle created a system for testing the soundness of an argument, which is like testing a theory in a science experiment. According to Aristotle, three elements work together to persuade a listener: ethos, pathos, and logos.

This photograph shows a statue of the philosopher Aristotle, who lived from 384 B.C. to 322 B.C.

Ethos refers to the credibility or believability of the speaker. You're more likely to believe information about chemical reactions when they come from your science teacher. Your history teacher may have correct scientific information, but you may be more confident about his historical information. A person's credibility, or ethos, is also established through attitude, posture, and confidence.

Pathos refers to the speaker's emotional intensity when talking about a subject. When a friend talks about her favorite new film, her attitude toward the film will be reflected not only in her words, but also in her gestures and tone of voice.

Logos refers to the logic or reasoning behind what a speaker says. You're more likely to convince your father that spending the night at your friend's house is a good idea if you can prove that you need the time to work with your friend on a school assignment.

The key to successful public speaking is to include all these elements in your speech. You have probably listened to an adult who has ethos, or credibility, but their lack of pathos, or enthusiasm, made you lose interest. Or you may have been unsatisfied with the explanations of emotional friends who could only say, "That's just how we feel!" If a speaker's reasons simply don't make sense, why listen?

As you develop a speech, you want to be sure you offer listeners information that is useful, accurate, and vivid. This doesn't mean you have to be a stand-up comic or a drama queen. Instead, you need to balance statistics with interesting stories. If you are thoroughly prepared and have rehearsed, the audience is more likely to believe you as well.

In a truly persuasive speech, the elements of ethos, pathos, and logos are all present.

Chapter 3

Preparing the Speech

Many times speakers are assigned a topic. If you are not assigned a topic, deciding on something that will be interesting for you and your audience may be difficult. Some issues appeal to certain audiences more than others. Students at your school may be concerned about the dress code or the lunch menu. Such topics are worthy of a speech for an audience of classmates, but may not interest a group of adults. Or you may feel strongly about the graphics for a particular video game, but a speech about the issue may not appeal to your peers. From another perspective, some topics are just not that exciting, even though they may be easy to research. Often students jump quickly to topics that seem effortless: drug use, automobile safety, teen issues. While these are worthy issues for discussion and a great deal of research is readily available, making the information interesting for your audience may be challenging.

With a topic like automobile safety, you may find the amount of information overwhelming. Therefore, you must narrow the topic to make it more manageable. Narrowing automobile safety down to something more specific can also make your speech more interesting. Here are some specific automobile safety topics.

- Every car should be equipped with side-impact airbags.
- Improved safety features are needed in sport-utility vehicles.
- More should be done to prevent vehicle fires.

Developing the Thesis

The thesis is the focus of your speech. It may be in the form of a sentence, like the examples above, or in the form of a question. The thesis needs to be specific and express the main idea. Phrasing your thesis in the form of a question may also make your topic more interesting.

- Should all cars be equipped with side-impact airbags?
- Will improved safety standards decrease deaths due to rollovers in sport-utility vehicles?
- Should the National Transportation Safety Board do more to regulate fire hazards in vehicles?

Whether you choose to present the thesis as a statement or a question, it should lay a clear and simple foundation for your speech.

Proving the Thesis

The next step in creating your speech is to decide how you can best prove your point. Organizing the speech requires

13

that you address the thesis and produce reasons to support your major argument. Consider the question asked at the beginning of this book: Should downloading music be a crime? There are only two possible answers: yes or no. In order to persuade the audience, you need to offer substantial reasons to support your answer. If you want to convince us that downloading music should or should not be a crime, what reasons might you offer?

In order to determine that, you will need to start with a first round of research. You may already feel strongly about the issue and have some clear reasons for your position. But without supporting information to back up your argument, you run the risk of having plenty of pathos, but no ethos or logos. Consider the following argument:

> Downloading music should be a crime because it decreases music sales. I have a friend in a band, and they recorded a CD that has been uploaded through file sharing. Their record isn't selling in stores because everyone can get it for free online. Does that seem fair?

Actually, it doesn't seem fair. However, this argument lacks any solid evidence to support the reasoning. Essentially, the argument that "music downloading decreases sales" is unsupported by any significant proof. Suppose you were to offer evidence from the Recording Industry Association of America (RIAA) about the impact of downloading on sales, in addition to offering the example of a friend's band. Then the audience might be convinced that, by decreasing sales, music downloads are theft. Therefore, the claims you make should be reinforced with research, information, and stories.

The first round of research may lead you to a different conclusion from your first reaction to the thesis. For example, some students make an effort to argue that they should not be required to take a foreign language. However, there is little research to support this position.

Citing Sources

Once you begin to gather research, some of it will become a part of your speech. Keep a list of each Web site, book, news article, or other media source you consult. Vary the types of sources from which you draw your material. The Internet is an excellent research tool. There are a variety of sources on the Web from which you can pull information. Newspapers and news organizations from around the world have online versions, too. However, you should also use books and scholarly articles from journals. Some schools and libraries may offer helpful resources, such as a journal service. Including information from books, magazines or journals, newspapers, and other sources increases the strength of your argument. This variety also demonstrates that you've taken the time to research a broad set of sources to help prove your point.

Your instructor may ask you to compile a bibliography, so you will need to keep track of all the sources you use. You must cite any source that you quote directly or paraphrase in your speech. Failure to cite your sources is plagiarism. You have an obligation to give credit to those individuals whose work you use. Just as downloading music is considered theft by the RIAA, using another person's work as your own is a form of stealing. Additionally, there is no shame in finding other individuals who agree with your position and citing them in your speech. Quotes from authorities will reinforce your ideas.

Instead of just talking about a friend's experience with downloaded music, a more convincing argument might sound something like this:

> According to the RIAA Web site, each year the industry loses about $4.2 billion to piracy worldwide: "We estimate we lose millions of dollars a day to all forms of piracy." As the band Tool noted, "Basically, it's about music—if you didn't create it, why should you exploit it? True fans don't rip off their artists." Downloading music for free is stealing. Respect for musicians and their work means that we as consumers and listeners have to pay for the music so our favorite artists can continue to produce new material.

This example credits both the RIAA Web site and the band Tool. Two experts agreeing with you increases your credibility, demonstrates clear reasoning, and adds an emotional appeal for Tool fans in your audience. Even if your audience members aren't Tool fans, they will appreciate the perspective of a famous band on the subject.

A note of caution concerning research: the Internet has revolutionized the amount of information available on any given topic, but you need to carefully consider the source. Sources may be biased. Even news organizations and scholarly journals may have unfair coverage of an issue. Editorialists can offer compelling arguments to support your position, but their political views may be considered extreme. Reading the "About Us" pages on Web sites or the biographical information about the author of an article or book may help you determine whether the source is biased or fair about a subject.

Patterns of Organization

After you begin researching for your speech, you may find yourself over-whelmed trying to decide what information you want to include. The next step in preparing your speech is to organize the information so that you prove your point, but don't repeat yourself. Compare the outlines below for a speech about testing.

Should students be required to pass standardized tests in order to graduate?

OUTLINE #1	OUTLINE #2
Yes, because . . .	Yes, because . . .
1. Standardized tests are the best measure of student achievement.	1. Standardized tests are the most efficient method for measuring learning.
2. Schools need to determine who ought to graduate.	2. Standardized tests provide a measure of school responsibility.
3. Everyone has an equal chance on a standardized test.	3. Standardized tests are the least biased means for determining who passes.

17

The main ideas for the first outline seem fine until you consider that to prove the first idea—standardized tests are the best measure of achievement—you have to include the second and third ideas. This will result in a very short speech with a lot of repetition about how testing is the best way to determine who graduates.

However, the second outline has three distinct points. Each point can be supported separately from the others. They are three reasons to require standardized testing as opposed to other ways to determine who graduates. Each reason can be independently researched and can stand alone in an effort to persuade your audience.

The reasons to oppose standardized testing are available, too. Saying "no" and defending that position on standardized testing is probably even more appealing to an audience of students.

Once you decide what you want to argue, there are a few standard methods to consider about how to organize your thoughts. The pattern used to organize the second standardized test outline is topical, meaning that each main idea addresses an issue related to the thesis.

A chronological pattern may be used if you are discussing changes occurring over time:

Thesis: Have we conquered racism in America?
1. Historical analysis
2. Current issues
3. Future concerns

A spatial pattern may be used if you need to talk about relationships in geography:

> **Thesis: Will building a fence along the U.S.-Mexico border decrease illegal immigration?**
> 1. California border issues
> 2. Arizona and New Mexico border issues
> 3. Texas border issues

A problem-solution pattern may be used if the speech poses a question that lends itself to potential solutions:

> **Thesis: Will building a fence along the U.S.-Mexico border decrease illegal immigration?**
> 1. Define the problem.
> 2. Discuss the causes.
> 3. Offer possible solutions.

For most topics, you can answer "yes" or "no," research the issues, and uncover any number of possible solutions that may or may not appeal to your audience.

A cause-effect pattern may be used to discuss why things happen and the results that are produced:

> **Thesis: Children should not be allowed to play violent video games.**
> 1. Witnessing game violence leads to aggressive behavior.
> 2. Witnessing game violence causes less sensitivity to violence.
> 3. Taking part in game violence leads to violent behavior.

With a cause-effect speech, you need to be certain the causes actually produce the claimed effects. Just because two things happen around the same time, or near one another, does not mean one caused the other. Some people believe that if they wash their cars, it will rain. The occurrence of rain is just chance. Similarly, many people believe witnessing game violence makes a person behave violently. It may be, however, that aggressive people are drawn to violent games. The research is mixed at best.

Whatever pattern you choose, the goal of your speech is to prove your position. The reasons you choose to confirm your thesis are more persuasive when they are supported by well-researched, clear arguments. Statistics, quotations from experts, and actual examples are more likely to convince your audience than made-up examples or personal views.

Final Construction

Once you have found research to support your thesis and have decided how to organize your points, it is time to begin crafting the speech. It is often best to begin by constructing the thesis and body of the speech. Once you have these, the introduction and conclusion usually follow naturally.

The introduction contains four essential elements: the hook, justifier, thesis, and preview. The hook is a way to pull your audience into the speech. It can be a news item, a shocking statistic, a quotation, a narrative, or some other creative way to catch your listeners' attention. You will probably find your hook during your initial research. The justifier is a sentence or two about the importance of the issue or topic. It links the topic to the audience in a more direct way. It may be helpful to consider why you found the topic to be important. The thesis is the focus of your speech and may be a sentence or a question. Finally, the preview introduces your audience to the reasons you will use to prove your point. Be sure to state your reasons in the same order you plan to discuss them to avoid confusing your audience.

The conclusion also contains four elements: the review, restatement of the thesis, impact, and wrap-up. The review of the main ideas is simply a reminder of what you have talked about in the speech. You also need to restate the thesis. Together, these two parts offer a summary of the speech for the audience. The impact statement is related to the justifier in the introduction. When attempting to persuade an audience, it is helpful to point out the effect of your position. Finally, you want to wrap up the speech with a statement, statistic, or story that ties the whole speech together.

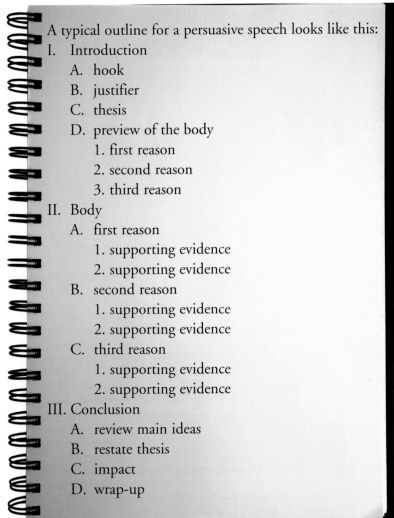

A typical outline for a persuasive speech looks like this:
I. Introduction
   A. hook
   B. justifier
   C. thesis
   D. preview of the body
      1. first reason
      2. second reason
      3. third reason
II. Body
   A. first reason
      1. supporting evidence
      2. supporting evidence
   B. second reason
      1. supporting evidence
      2. supporting evidence
   C. third reason
      1. supporting evidence
      2. supporting evidence
III. Conclusion
   A. review main ideas
   B. restate thesis
   C. impact
   D. wrap-up

The example on page 23—a topical pattern—illustrates a well-developed outline. This outline is meant to demonstrate the amount of research and effort necessary to create a solid speech. For delivery purposes, however, too much information is included. An outline with this much information may encourage a speaker to read to the audience, instead of talking to them about the issues. The next two chapters discuss how to deliver a speech for a general audience in a competition.

A variety of sources is needed to produce a well-crafted persuasive argument.

TOPICAL PATTERN

I. Introduction
   A. According to CNN Online, the number of illegal immigrants from Mexico is growing at about 300,000 per year, as reported by census figures and the former Immigration and Naturalization Service.
   B. Congress is currently debating what to do about the increasing number of illegal immigrants, specifically those from Mexico. Proposals range from forgiveness for many already living in the United States to building a fence or wall to prevent illegal entry into the country from Mexico.
   C. Will building a fence along the U.S.-Mexico border stop illegal immigration?
   D. No, because many obstacles stand in the way of such a simple solution.
     1. Legal immigration is too difficult.
     2. Illegal routes for entry will shift.
     3. Illegal immigrants include more than Mexicans.

II. Body
   A. Legal immigration is too difficult.
     1. As an American citizen who understands English, I visited the U.S. Center for Immigration Services Web site to determine how to apply to live legally in this country. It's not clear. You must file any number of forms, and the cost for each one ranges from $78 for a fingerprint check to $1,000 for permanent residency.
     2. For citizens of other nations who are classified as "unskilled" labor, the process is expensive and difficult to navigate without the services of an expert. Any number of lawyers can help, but all services come with a fee.
   B. Illegal immigration routes will shift.
     1. The Border Patrol has already seen a shift in immigration routes from Texas and California to New Mexico and Arizona. This shift has led to an increased number of deaths as immigrants attempt to cross desert areas as opposed to the more populated and highly patrolled areas of border towns.
     2. If the borders become too difficult to navigate, alternative routes will be created. An article in the *San Francisco Chronicle* quoted Maria Echaveste, an immigration expert at the Center for American Progress, a research group in Washington, D.C. Echaveste said, "People will seek other ways to come into the country. I suspect more use of water, more use of [fake] documents, more use of criminal smuggling."
   C. Illegal immigrants include more than Mexicans.
     1. The number of unauthorized immigrants to the United States remained more or less steady from 1996 to 2005, according to population expert Jeff Passel of the Pew Hispanic Center in Washington, D.C. He said 700,000 to 750,000 people enter the country illegally each year, helping raise the total to a record 11 million illegal immigrants in 2005. Up to one-third of those 11 million people did not walk across the border illegally. They entered the country on tourist, student, or work visas and simply stayed after their visa expired, Passel said. These visa "overstays" are from China, the Philippines, India, South America, Canada, Ireland, and many other countries, said Passel, whose estimates are used by the Department of Homeland Security.
     2. According to *The Times of India*, reporting on the recent arrest of 2,100 illegal immigrants, "Homeland Security Secretary Michael Chertoff said the [arrests were] part of a 'new and tough' enforcement strategy that includes worksite enforcement and a crackdown on the criminal [systems] that [bring about] illegal immigration. The fugitives arrested in the operation came from dozens of countries, including Bangladesh, Brazil, China, Indonesia, Iraq, Pakistan, and United Kingdom."

III. Conclusion
   A. Since . . .
     1. Legal immigration is too difficult;
     2. Illegal immigration routes will shift;
     3. And illegal immigrants include more than Mexican citizens;
   B. Building a fence along the U.S.-Mexico border will not stop illegal immigration.
   C. The United States must alter its immigration policy to better serve American businesses that need the services of immigrants and those who wish to immigrate legally. Decreasing illegal immigration into this country will take more than building a wall or targeting one particular group.
   D. Writer Anthony Walton's words should remind us that the United States can help the immigrants of tomorrow: "America's greatest strength, and its greatest weakness, is our belief in second chances, our belief that we can always start over, that things can be made better."

23

Chapter 4

Delivering the Speech

Did you know that many adults list public speaking as one of their greatest fears? Similarly, many students prefer to hand in a paper rather than stand in front of an audience and say the same things aloud. There are reasons why this is true. One may be that we—as viewers of the modern media—have very high standards for public speaking. News reporters, comedians, and actors make public speaking seem both simple and intimidating. Another reason is that students do not receive as many opportunities to stand up and speak as they do to write essays. The good news is that you can overcome a fear of speaking in front of people. How? Practice!

Basketball players and ballet dancers make their activities seem effortless through countless hours of preparation. So, too, does the effective public speaker. Just as athletes and dancers get nervous before performances, speakers can also be uneasy. A nervous rush of adrenaline can result in what is known as the "fight-or-flight response." When you are in a situation that produces anxiety, it may seem easier to run away than to stand up and speak. Over time, if you practice and perform often, the nervousness will lessen and you will become more comfortable in front of people.

Voice

Your voice and the way you speak reveal a lot about you. This is another reason why some people avoid public speaking. Think about speakers you have seen on television or in a live situation. As you watch and listen, you make judgments about their knowledge and about them. People who speak with flawed grammar or heavy accents are sometimes viewed less positively than those who speak in a standard style with less of an accent.

Related to the accent and grammar of someone's speech are their tone of voice and the variety of their vocal range. Individuals who speak in one tone or in a high-pitched voice sound less pleasing than speakers who are more animated and less shrill. Most people are not aware of how they sound to others because we hear our voice from inside our own head. The best way to know how you sound is to make a recording of your voice and play it back. You may be surprised at how your voice sounds from this different perspective. If there are things you do not like about your accent, your pitch, or your tone, you can work to improve or change those aspects.

Another feature of the voice is rate, or how fast you speak. Scientific studies show that the rate at which you speak is related to the rate at which you think, which can be good or bad. If you speak so quickly that you stumble or stutter while speaking, slowing down is absolutely necessary. If you fill space with "uh" and "um," this may reveal that you are searching for something to say. The key is to speak quickly enough to show that you are knowledgeable and slowly enough so that the audience can easily understand you.

Diction

Diction includes both the words you choose and how you pronounce them. One of the confusing aspects of public speaking is that it is usually less formal than the way you write, but more formal than the way you chat with your friends. So choosing your words wisely and speaking them well impacts the way your speech—and you—are perceived.

Dental work such as braces and retainers creates many diction problems for students. Speech teachers usually have vocal exercises, including tongue twisters, that you can use to help you overcome the limitations created by your dental work.

Other diction problems arise simply from being lazy while speaking. Mumbling, mushy-sounding words, words that seem to be missing beginnings, middles, or endings—the list is endless. One problem listeners find annoying is the dreaded "filler" word. Repeating words and phrases such as "like," "you know," and "also" interrupts the flow of ideas.

The best way to correct issues with diction in a public speaking situation is to correct them in your everyday speech. You should practice speaking well while having conversations with your friends at lunch, with your parents in the car, or in classroom discussions. Conquering bad speech habits will improve your performance in public speaking situations, as well as in everyday communication.

Gestures

Public speaking would be very boring if every speaker were just a talking head. Even though the speakers we see on the news are sitting fairly still, they have lively faces and sometimes gesture with their hands.

When this speaker outstretches his arms, he emphasizes an important part of his speech.

Comedians and actors rarely stand perfectly still while they talk to an audience. If you observe your teachers closely, most of them probably move while they are conducting lectures or discussions.

Gestures add life and interest to speeches. They are meant for emphasis and illustration. However, gestures should be limited in range and frequen-

This speaker seems more passionate about his speech because of his gestures and facial expressions.

cy. Imagine a box in front of you. Your chin rests on the top, the bottom edge is the height of your hips, and the sides are at the width of your elbows when your hands are placed on your hips. This "gesture box" is where your gestures should be aimed. If you gesture above your chin, your hands may block the view of your face or the sound of your words. Gestures below hip level make you look like a penguin. Gestures wider than the width of your extended elbows are too broad and overly dramatic.

By limiting the frequency of your gestures, you avoid "talking with your hands." You've probably noticed people who can't have a conversation without moving their hands. Constant gesturing prevents a speaker from emphasizing or illustrating specific points because the speaker seems to be emphasizing everything. It is no different from having an instant-message chat with someone who has the caps lock on. IT SEEMS LIKE YELLING AND NOTHING STANDS OUT AS IMPORTANT.

Though you should limit the range and frequency of your gestures, be sure to use some gestures. Standing still while speaking is uncomfortable and makes you seem nervous or tense. People naturally gesture while speaking.

Movement

Movement beyond gestures may include the use of a podium, or walking while speaking. If you have access to a podium, be sure the height of the podium allows the audience to see you clearly. If you're short, you may need to either stand on something in order to be seen or consider not using the podium. Public speakers like to use a podium if they have extensive notes and don't wish to hold them throughout the speech. The podium is a tool, not a crutch. Avoid leaning on it, gripping it until your hands hurt, banging on it for emphasis, or hiding behind it. Stand back from the podium and use it merely as a resting place for your notes. You still need to gesture and make eye contact with your audience.

You may wish to consider walking while speaking. Walking during a speech allows you to demonstrate physically a shift you're making verbally. Usually, speakers move during the shifts from the introduction into the first main idea, then to the second idea, the third, and finally the conclusion. The main issue when walking is to be aware of your audience. Do not pace. Pacing draws the audience's attention away from the words and makes a speaker seem nervous. Walk so that you are able to see the audience and they are able to see you.

Whether you walk or use the podium, the key to maintaining control of your body while speaking is planting your feet. You should plant your feet squarely under your shoulders with your toes pointing forward. Doing so prevents you from rocking or shifting around while standing in place. Planting your feet also improves your posture and encourages you to hold your head up, which increases your ability to make yourself heard and gives the impression of confidence.

Projecting Confidence

At this point, the thought of making a speech may seem overwhelming. You have a list of things to do and not to do, but your "fight-or-flight response" is screaming "Run away!" There are two simple things that project confidence to the audience and will allow you to overcome your concerns about speaking well.

First, know your subject. The primary issue that creates fear in public speaking is a lack of knowledge. If you've taken the time to do the research and prepare your speech, you can use the adrenaline in your bloodstream to your advantage. When

This speaker uses the podium as a place to rest his notes.

you're confident in your knowledge and understanding of a subject, you have no need to fear the audience.

Practice your speech aloud in front of friends to gain confidence.

You must also practice speaking aloud. Reading what you have written in your outline over and over produces familiarity with the content but is not the same thing as practicing speaking. Practicing out loud at a normal volume and pace is important.

Second, make eye contact with your audience. Studies in communication reveal that 85 percent of our expression occurs in the region of our forehead, eyebrows, and eyes. Think about a conversation with someone. How do you know if they are lying? Someone who avoids looking at you is suspicious. Eye contact demonstrates honesty, knowledge, and confidence. When speaking to an audience, either in the classroom or in a larger location, it's necessary to make eye contact with each person in the room—or each area of the room—so that people feel you are speaking to them

The preparation you do in researching your subject, creating the speech, practicing it aloud, and delivering it will inspire you to continue improving your public speaking skills. Skill in public communication is essential to success in business and professional life. Taking the time to develop good communication skills will improve your chances for achieving your goals in the future.

Chapter 5

Competitive Extemporaneous Speaking

You have now learned how to create a well-structured argument and how to present that argument to an audience. Students who enjoy this often consider joining their school's speech-and-debate team, sometimes called forensic club. "Forensic" simply means "suitable to courts of law or to public discussion and debate." Forensic competitors do not examine bodies or test DNA. Forensic competitors utilize the skills necessary to communicate successfully, whether they're in a court of law talking about legal issues or with friends discussing current events. For middle and high school competition, a range of events in performance, debate, and public speaking are included. Extemporaneous speaking, or extemp, is among these.

Rules and Guidelines

Individual states vary in their rules and guidelines for extemp. At the national level, though, the rules for extemp are fairly standard. For this reason, this chapter will focus on the national competition rules.

The National Forensic League (NFL) divides extemp into two categories: domestic and international. The domestic category refers to matters within the country, such as U.S. policy and politics (including social issues such as education and health care), economic issues surrounding commerce between states, U.S. foreign policy, military and security issues, and other political concerns.

The international category is much more extensive and requires students to be familiar with all continents; international organizations such as the United Nations and the European Union; and international political, social, and economic issues. It shares the issue of U.S. foreign policy with the domestic category, but otherwise the two areas are fairly distinct.

The most successful competitors in extemp compete in both domestic and international extemp. Some local or state tournaments have combined extemp where the rounds alternate between foreign and domestic. Some tournaments allow students to enter both divisions.

The basic rules state that you have 30 minutes to prepare a 7-minute speech. You may have printed, published files in order to prepare (including books, magazines, newspapers, news articles, and scholarly journals). Students are allowed to draw three topics and choose one. Time begins when a student is called to draw. Once a topic is chosen, the student returns to their files to prepare the speech, which is delivered to a judge at the conclusion of preparation, or prep, time. No notes may be used while delivering the speech.

Consultation and conversation between teammates or

competitors are not allowed during prep time. Prewritten speeches or outlines are not allowed in the prep room, and the tournament staff may search the files of anyone accused of breaking the rules.

Before the fight-or-flight response starts urging you to run again, have confidence that you can learn the skills to become a successful competitor. Again, knowledge and preparation are keys to success. The best way to improve knowledge is through the creation of extensive, quality files.

Building an Extemp File

Extemp files are generally carried about in large boxes or "tubs." Since the files are full of paper, they are quite heavy. But when they are well maintained, the files can stay manageable and useful.

First, you need a system for setting up the information so that articles can be located quickly. An index is the best place to start. Many extemp teams already have a list of areas that are in their files and frequently will share. In the event that you're starting completely from scratch, a sample of an index is shown at the end of this chapter.

Once you have the index, you need to create a system for filing the articles you locate. Color-coding folders is a simple way to visually organize by subject areas. For instance, all the file folders for African nations might be green. You can further organize by making labels a different color print or different font style for each region of the continent. The system is only as complicated as you make it.

Getting your extemp team together to talk about issues is a great way to build knowledge.

After folders are labeled and organized—either regionally or alphabetically by issue, or both—you need to start filling them with information. You may do this by cutting articles out of newspapers, including your local paper. If you cut articles out of the paper, write the date and name of the newspaper on each article. It's also advisable to keep multiple-page articles together by either pasting them onto a single sheet of paper or stapling the pages together. Downloading articles from online news organizations like Reuters, CNN, or the Associated Press is also acceptable. If you download articles from the Internet, make sure they have the Web address on them, as required by National Forensic League rules.

It's almost impossible for one person to build an extensive set of files for extemp. This is where a team comes in. Dividing the work by subject area will allow the entire group to make better use of their research time. Getting together after school to file all the articles is an opportunity to discuss the articles and issues as you file them by subject.

If your team also receives magazines, journals, and newspapers, these need to be systematically filed. Different issues of the same magazine can be put into spiral binders or kept together in a box. For instance, all the issues of *The Economist* or *The Atlantic* are placed in one box, stacked with the most recent issue on top. The best extemp files are well maintained, which means that every tournament week, the oldest files are removed and more recent articles are added. Maintaining files requires discipline. Otherwise, you may find yourself with a question you cannot answer because you have no information in the tubs.

Sample Index

COMMUNICATION / TECHNOLOGY (CO)
CO: Computers
CO: Computers - Privacy Issues
CO: Copyright Law
CO: Cyberterrorism/Hackers
CO: Federal Communications Commission (FCC)
CO: Internet
CO: Internet - Access
CO: Internet - Companies
CO: Internet - Day Trading
CO: Internet - E-Commerce
CO: Internet - Regulation
CO: Internet - Stocks
CO: Internet - Taxes
CO: Microsoft
CO: Postal Service
CO: Radio
CO: Telephones
CO: Television

DEFENSE/MILITARY (DF)
DF: General
DF: Air Force
DF: Army
DF: Ballistic Missiles/NMD
DF: Biological Weapons
DF: Central Intelligence Agency (CIA)
DF: Chemical Weapons
DF: Coast Guard
DF: Conventional Weapons - General
DF: Espionage
DF: Homeland Security Department
DF: Marines
DF: Military Bases
DF: Military Policies
DF: Military Readiness
DF: National Security
DF: Navy
DF: Nuclear Arms
DF: Pentagon/Joint Chiefs of Staff
DF: Recruitment/Shortage
DF: Secretary of Defense
DF: Spending
DF: Terrorism
DF: Terrorism - Cyberattacks
DF: Treaties

DOMESTIC ECONOMY (DE)
DE: General
DE: Banking
DE: Bankruptcy
DE: Bonds
DE: Budget Surplus
DE: Consumer Confidence/Spending
DE: Consumer Debt/Credit Cards
DE: Economic Growth
DE: Federal Deficit/Debt
DE: Federal Reserve Board/Greenspan
DE: Federal Reserve Board - Interest Rates
DE: Inflation
DE: Internal Revenue Service (IRS)
DE: Rich/Poor Gap
DE: Savings
DE: Securities and Exchange Commission (SEC)
DE: Stock Market
DE: Taxes
DE: Trade Deficit
DE: Treasury
DE: Treasury Bills
DE: Unemployment
DE: Wages
DE: Wages - Minimum Wage
DE: Wages - Women

EDUCATION (ED)
ED: General
ED: Academic Standards
ED: Bilingual Education
ED: Curriculum
ED: Curriculum - Evolution
ED: Curriculum - Sex Education
ED: Dropouts
ED: Funding
ED: Higher Education
ED: Higher Education - Academic Freedom
ED: Higher Education - Costs
ED: Home Schooling
ED: Minorities
ED: Parental Involvement
ED: Reform
ED: Schools - Buildings
ED: Schools - Overcrowding
ED: Schools - Safety
ED: Teachers - Pay
ED: Teachers - Shortage/Recruitment
ED: Teachers - Training Tests
ED: Vouchers

ENERGY (EG)
EG: General
EG: Coal
EG: Companies
EG: Department of Energy
EG: Electricity
EG: Energy Crisis
EG: Ethanol
EG: Gasoline
EG: Gasoline - Prices
EG: Hydropower
EG: Nuclear
EG: Nuclear - Waste
EG: Oil - OPEC
EG: Oil - Prices
EG: Oil - Supply
EG: Solar
EG: Wind

ENVIRONMENT (EV)
EV: General
EV: Acid Rain
EV: Air Pollution
EV: Army Corps of Engineers
EV: Department of Interior
EV: Disasters
EV: Disasters - FEMA
EV: Drought
EV: Endangered Species
EV: Environmental Protection Agency (EPA)
EV: Forests/Parks/Ecosystems
EV: Global Warming
EV: Global Warming - Kyoto Protocol
EV: Landfills
EV: Soil - Contamination
EV: Soil - Erosion
EV: Water
EV: Water - Pollution
EV: Weather
EV: Wildfires

HEALTH (HE)
HE: General
HE: AIDS/HIV
HE: Alcohol
HE: Alternative Medicine
HE: Cancer
HE: Costs
HE: Disease
HE: Disease - CDC
HE: Drugs - Herbal
HE: Drugs - Over the Counter
HE: Drug Use/Treatment
HE: Elderly Care
HE: Food & Drug Administration (FDA)
HE: Food Safety
HE: Genetics
HE: HMOs/Managed Care
HE: Immunizations
HE: Insurance
HE: Medical Marijuana
HE: Medical Safety
HE: Medical Technology/Procedures
HE: Medicare/Medicaid
HE: Mental Health
HE: National Institutes of Health
HE: Neonatal Care
HE: Nurse Shortage
HE: Nursing Home
HE: Organ Transplants
HE: Patients Bill of Rights
HE: Prescription Drugs
HE: Prescription Drugs - Children
HE: Prescription Drugs - Elderly
HE: Tobacco
HE: Veterans' Health
HE: Workplace Safety/OSHA
HE: Women's Health

IMMIGRATION (IM)
IM: General
IM: Amnesty/Asylum
IM: Deportation
IM: High-Skilled Workers
IM: Illegal
IM: Illegal - Border Patrol
IM: INS
IM: Refugees

39

INDUSTRY/LABOR (IN)
IN: General
IN: Agriculture
IN: Cola Wars
IN: Entertainment/Media
IN: Federal Trade Commission (FTC)
IN: Firearms
IN: Hotels
IN: Insurance
IN: Mergers
IN: Mergers - AOL/Time Warner
IN: Pharmaceuticals
IN: Real Estate
IN: Retail
IN: Small Business
IN: Steel
IN: Sweatshops
IN: Telecommunications
IN: Unions
IN: Unions - AFL/CIO
IN: Unions - Strikes
IN: Unions - UAW
IN: Work Force
IN: Working Conditions

JUDICIAL BRANCH (JD)
JD: General
JD: Attorney General
JD: Federal Courts
JD: Nominations
JD: Supreme Court

LAW ENFORCEMENT (LW)
LW: General
LW: Alchohol, Tobacco, and Firearms (ATF)
LW: Child Abduction
LW: Child Abuse
LW: Crime
LW: Crime - Juvenile
LW: Crime - White Collar
LW: DNA
LW: Domestic Violence
LW: Drunk Driving
LW: Due Process
LW: Due Process - Car Searches
LW: Due Process - Miranda
LW: Federal Bureau of Investigation (FBI)
LW: Hate Crimes
LW: Militias
LW: Police
LW: Police Corruption - LA
LW: Police Corruption - NY
LW Prisons
LW: Racial Profiling
LW: War on Drugs

LEGISLATIVE BRANCH (LG)
LG: General
LG: Bipartisanship
LG: Budget
LG: Budget Surplus/CBO
LG: Campaign Finance Reform
LG: Census
LG: Congressional Budget Office (CBO)
LG: D.C. Statehood
LG: Democrats
LG: Fast Track Authority
LG: Foreign Aid
LG: Foreign Policy
LG: Government Accountability Office
LG: House of Representatives
LG: Independent Counsels
LG: Republicans
LG: Senate
LG: Special Interest Groups
LG: Taxes
LG: Term Limits
LG: Trade Issues

POLITICS/ELECTIONS (PO)
PO: General
PO: Campaign Finance
PO: Congress - General
PO: Congress - Hillary Clinton
PO: Democrats
PO: President - General
PO: Republicans
PO: Reform Party
PO: Reform Party Leadership Issues
PO: Reform Party - Perot
PO: Third Parties
PO: Voting Reform/Electoral College

SOCIAL ISSUES (SO)
SO: Abortion
SO: Affirmative Action
SO: Animal Rights
SO: Anthrax
SO: Awards
SO: Capital Punishment
SO: Censorship
SO: Child Support/Welfare
SO: Confederate Flag
SO: Disabled/Handicapped
SO: Drug Legalization
SO: Drug Testing
SO: English Only
SO: Flag Burning
SO: Free Speech
SO: Gambling
SO: Gay and Lesbian Rights
SO: Gender
SO: Gun Control
SO: Hate Groups
SO: Homeless
SO: Housing
SO: Native Americans
SO: Native Americans - Casinos
SO: Population/Demographics
SO: Poverty
SO: Privacy
SO: Racism
SO: Religion
SO: Religious Right
SO: Right to Die/Euthanasia
SO: School Prayer
SO: Sexual Harassment
SO: Social Security
SO: Sports
SO: Suburban Sprawl
SO: Violence
SO: Violence - Media
SO: Welfare

SPACE (SP)
SP: General
SP: Hubble Telescope
SP: NASA
SP: NASA - Budget
SP: NASA - Problems
SP: Planets
SP: Planets - Exploration
SP: Satellites
SP: Shuttle Missions
SP: Space Station

TRANSPORTATION (TP)
TP: General
TP: Airlines
TP: Airlines - FAA
TP: Airlines - Production
TP: Airlines - Safety
TP: Airports
TP: Automobiles
TP: Automobiles - Road Congestion
TP: Automobiles - Road Rage
TP: Automobiles - Tire Recall
TP: National Transportation Safety Board (NTSB)
TP: Office of National Airline Security
TP: Railroads
TP: Railroads - AMTRAK
TP: Ships
TP: Trucking

WORLD AFFAIRS/ORGANIZATIONS (WO)
WO: Human Rights
WO: Hunger/Poverty
WO: Land Mines
WO: NATO
WO: Nuclear Proliferation
WO: Peace Corps
WO: Population
WO: Red Cross
WO: Terrorism
WO: United Nations
WO: United Nations - U.S. Relations
WO: United Nations - War Crimes
WO: World Court
WO: World Health Organization (WHO)

AFRICA (AF)
AF: General
AF: General - AIDS
AF: General - Organizations
AF: Algeria
AF: Angola
AF: Botswana
AF: Burundi
AF: Chad
AF: Congo - Brazzaville
AF: Democratic Republic of Congo
AF: Egypt
AF: Eritrea
AF: Ethiopia
AF: Ghana
AF: Ivory Coast (Côte d'Ivoire)

AF: Kenya
AF: Kenya - Economy
AF: Kenya - Politics
AF: Liberia
AF: Libya
AF: Mali
AF: Morocco
AF: Mozambique
AF: Nigeria
AF: Rwanda
AF: Senegal
AF: Sierra Leone
AF: Somalia
AF: South Africa
AF: South Africa - Economy
AF: South Africa - Politics
AF: Sudan
AF: Uganda
AF: Zambia
AF: Zimbabwe

ASIA (AS)
AS: General
AS: General - Tsunami Relief
AS: Afghanistan
AS: Afghanistan - Politics
AS: Australia
AS: Bangladesh
AS: Cambodia
AS: China
AS: China - Economy
AS: China - Foreign Relations
AS: China - Government
AS: China - Hong Kong
AS: China - Human Rights/Religion
AS: China - Military
AS: China - Taiwan Relations
AS: China - Tibet
AS: China - U.S. Relations
AS: Georgia
AS: India
AS: India - Economy
AS: India - Politics
AS: Indonesia
AS: Indonesia - Economy
AS: Indonesia - Politics
AS: Japan
AS: Japan - Economy
AS: Japan - Foreign Relations
AS: Japan - Politics
AS: Malaysia
AS: Myanmar
AS: Nepal
AS: New Zealand
AS: North Korea
AS: North/South Korea Conflict
AS: Pacific Islands
AS: Pakistan
AS: Pakistan/India Conflict - Kashmir
AS: Philippines
AS: Philippines - Politics
AS: South Korea
AS: Sri Lanka
AS: 'Stans'
AS: Taiwan
AS: Thailand
AS: Vietnam

CARIBBEAN (CB)
CB: General
CB: Cuba
CB: Cuba - Trade
CB: Cuba - U.S. Relations
CB: Dominican Republic
CB: Jamaica
CB: Puerto Rico

EUROPE, EASTERN (EE)
EE: Balkans - Other
EE: Bosnia and Herzegovina
EE: Croatia
EE: Poland
EE: Romania
EE: Serbia and Montenegro
EE: Ukraine

EUROPE, WESTERN (EU)
EU: General
EU: England
EU: England - Economy
EU: England - Politics
EU: European Union
EU: European Union - Economy
EU: European Union - Foreign Relations
EU: European Union - Military
EU: European Union - Politics
EU: France
EU: France - Economy
EU: France - Politics
EU: Germany
EU: Germany - Economy
EU: Germany - Politics
EU: Greece
EU: Ireland
EU: Ireland - Peace Process
EU: Italy
EU: Netherlands
EU: Spain

GLOBAL ECONOMY (GE)
GE: General
GE: Currency
GE: Currency - Euro
GE: European Economic Institutions
GE: G-7/G-8 (Poor Russia)
GE: Globalization
GE: International Monetary Fund (IMF)
GE: NAFTA
GE: Trade - General
GE: World Bank
GE: World Trade Organization (WTO)

MIDDLE EAST (ME)
ME: General
ME: Cyprus
ME: Iran
ME: Iran - Economy
ME: Iran - Politics
ME: Iraq
ME: Iraq - Economy
ME: Iraq - Foreign Relations
ME: Iraq - Government
ME: Iraq - U.S. Relations
ME: Israel

ME: Israel - Government
ME: Israel - Social Issues
ME: Jordan
ME: Kuwait
ME: Lebanon
ME: Palestine
ME: Palestine - Politics
ME: Peace - General
ME: Peace - Israel/Palestine
ME: Peace - Israel/Palestine Foreign Help
ME: Saudi Arabia
ME: Saudi Arabia - Politics
ME: Syria
ME: Turkey
ME: Turkey - Kurds
ME: Yemen

NORTH AMERICA (NA)
NA: General
NA: Canada
NA: Canada - Economy
NA:: Canada - Politics
NA: Canada - Quebec
NA: El Salvador
NA: Guatemala
NA: Haiti
NA: Mexico
NA: Mexico - Economy
NA: Mexico - Politics
NA: Mexico - U.S. Relations
NA: Nicaragua
NA: Panama

RUSSIA (RU)
RU: General
RU: Chechnya
RU: Economy
RU: Foreign Relations
RU: Foreign Relations - U.S.
RU: Military
RU: Politics

SOUTH AMERICA (SA)
SA: General
SA: General - Economy
SA: Argentina
SA: Argentina - Economy
SA: Brazil
SA: Brazil - Economy
SA: Brazil - Politics
SA: Chile
SA: Colombia
SA: Ecuador
SA: Peru
SA: Venezuela
SA: Venezuela - Economy
SA: Venezuela - Politics

41

Chapter 6

Strategies for Success

Beyond understanding the rules and building files, there are a number of things an extemporaneous competitor can do to improve their chances for success. Begin with building a knowledge base. Read national or international newspapers or magazines regularly. Watch and listen to the news. Pay attention in your classes. Ask questions. Use the adults around you as a resource to understand current issues and events.

When you have more information and a greater understanding of world events, extemp becomes far easier. Also, you will find you have a greater interest in world affairs and will want to convey your opinions to others. Extemporaneous speaking is a great way to do this.

The most effective preparation for an extemporaneous event is practice. Before attending a tournament, practice preparing a speech in the standard 30-minute time frame. Have your own timer, and read and write for no more than 15 minutes. This will leave you enough time to practice the speech twice before delivering it to a critic. Practice in front of a teammate, teacher, or parent. You can also videotape the speech so you can review and evaluate your own performance.

At the tournament, dress and conduct yourself professionally. Half the battle in competition is presentation. If you look like a young reporter, the critic will respond more positively to your speech. If and when you're eliminated from competition in a tournament, watch the students who are continuing. You'll discover what they're doing to be successful and can use this information as you practice and prepare for future tournaments.

After your first tournament, try not to be discouraged if you didn't do as well as you had hoped. Each of us has to start somewhere, and you should use the evaluation you receive to help you improve. Continued focus on building your knowledge base—while practicing writing and delivery—will eventually lead to improvement and success.

Whether engaging others in argument or demonstrating your knowledge of a subject, the skills required for extemporaneous speaking are the most useful and universal of all forensic events. Success is created from combining both preparation and practice into a capable demonstration of knowledge and skill. Creating persuasive arguments based on solid logic and good research is a beneficial tool for students no matter what path they pursue later in life.

Glossary

adrenaline A chemical in the body that raises blood pressure and causes a rapid heartbeat when the body experiences stress or danger.

bibliography A list of books and articles used when writing that appears at the end of the text.

cause-effect pattern An outline arrangement that addresses the reasons a problem exists and its resulting impacts.

chronological pattern An outline arrangement that addresses events in order based on time.

diction The way in which words are spoken, including the words chosen and how those words are pronounced.

editorialist A journalist who writes about their opinion or view.

justifier A statement in a speech's introduction that relates the importance of the topic to the audience.

paraphrase To restate using different words.

perspective A viewpoint of a situation.

piracy Taking and using copyrighted materials without legal right.

plagiarism Copying another's writing or idea and presenting it as one's own.

podium A stand for a speaker to rest their notes on.

posture The way a person holds their body, especially while standing.

problem-solution pattern An outline arrangement that addresses an issue and its causes and offers possible solutions.

scholarly Relating to a source with a great deal of knowledge about a subject.

spatial pattern An outline arrangement that addresses an issue in terms of geography.

standardized test A test that measures a student's ability in comparison to an accepted standard.

statistics Facts and figures.

visa Permission given in a passport that allows a person to travel from or to a country.

For More Information

National Forensic League
125 Watson Street
P.O. Box 38
Ripon, WI 54971
Phone: (920) 748-6206
Web site: http://www.nflonline.org

**National Federation of State
    High School Associations**
P.O. Box 690
Indianapolis, IN 46206
Phone: (317) 972-6900
Web site: http://www.nfhs.org

**International Debate
    Education Association**
400 West 59th Street
New York, NY 10019
Phone: (212) 548-0185
Web site: http:/www.idebate.org

Web Sites

Due to the changing nature of Internet links, the Rosen Publishing Group, Inc., has developed an online list of Web sites related to the subject of this book. This site is updated regularly. Please use this link to access the list:
http://www.rosenlinks.com/psd/pesp

For Further Reading

Lynn, Dorothy, and Jessica Selasky. *Your Public Speaking Workout: Exercise Your Body Parts.* Boca Raton, FL: Funny Management Publishing, 2000.

McDaniel, Rebecca. *Scared Speechless: Public Speaking Step by Step.* Thousand Oaks, CA: Sage Publications, 1994.

Meany, John, and Kate Shuster. *Speak Out! Debate and Public Speaking in the Middle Grades.* New York: IDEA Press, 2005.

The Princeton Language Institute and Lenny Laskowski. *10 Days to More Confident Public Speaking.* New York: Warner Books, 2001.

Bibliography

Frieden, Terry. "INS: 7 Million Illegal Immigrants in United States." CNN.com/U.S., February 1, 2003. Retrieved July 2, 2006 (http://www.cnn.com/2003/US/01/31/illegal.immigration).

Hendricks, Tyche. "Border Security or Boondoggle? A Plan for 700 Miles of Mexican Border Wall Heads for Senate—Its Future Is Not Assured." *San Francisco Chronicle*, February 26, 2006. Retrieved July 2, 2006 (http://www.sfgate.com/cgi-bin/article.cgi?f=/c/a/2006/02/26/MNGHIHDUQF1.DTL&hw=border+security+boondoggle&sn=001&sc=1000).

Passel, Jeffrey S. "Size and Characteristics of the Unauthorized Migrant Population in the U.S.: Estimates Based on the March 2005 Current Population Survey." Pew Hispanic Center: Reports and Fact Sheets, March 7, 2006. Retrieved July 2, 2006 (http://pewhispanic.org/reports/report.php?ReportID=61).

Times of India, The. "Over 2,100 Illegal Immigrants Held in US." *The Times of India*, June 15, 2006. Retrieved July 2, 2006 (http://timesofindia.indiatimes.com/articleshow/1649820.cms).

U.S. Citizenship and Immigration Services. Retrieved July 2, 2006 (http://www.uscis.gov/graphics/index.htm).

Quotations Page, The. "Quotations by Author: Anthony Walton." Retrieved July 2, 2006 (http://www.quotationspage.com/quotes/Anthony_Walton/).

Index

About the Author

Dixie Waldo is the Director of Forensics at West Des Moines Valley High School in Iowa. In 12 years of coaching, more than fifty of her high school students reached the NFL National Tournament, including four finalists and a national champion. Before moving to Iowa, Waldo qualified over 100 students to the Texas Forensic Association State Tournament, including the 2005 State Champion Team and the three-time State Champion in International Extemp. Waldo holds a master's degree in Communication Studies from the University of North Texas.

Photo Credits

Cover, pp. 11, 27, 28, 31, 32, 37 Courtesy of the National Forensic League; p. 9 © Getty Images; p. 17, 21, 22, 23, 36 © Shutterstock.

Designer: Haley Wilson
Editor: Therese Shea